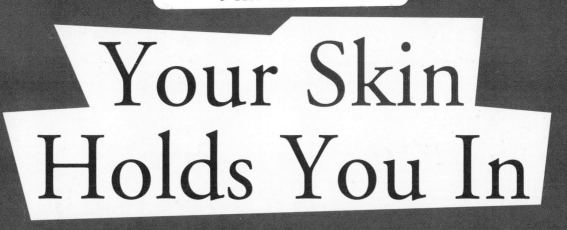

Your Skin Holds You In

A Book About Your Skin

BY

BECKY **BAINES**

 NATIONAL GEOGRAPHIC

Washington, D.C.

Skin can come in different colors.

Skin color comes from a pigment called melanin.

The more melanin you have,
the darker your skin.

And then those colors can change!

brrrrr.
rosy cheeks

Your skin warms

A layer of fat under your skin keeps your insides a toasty 98.6 degrees.

8

you up,

Your skin cools you down, with sweat that's wet like rain.

As wet skin dries, heat is pulled from your body.

sweat

sweat

sweat

Your skin has holes!

The tiniest holes on your skin are called pores.

hole

hole

two tiny holes

big hole

And hair!   # And spots!

hair

hair

nose hair—eew!

spots

freckles are spots of
melanin on your skin

hair

11

day two

ouch!

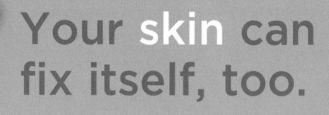

Your **skin** can fix itself, too.

Under this scab your body is making new skin.

day six

day twelve

new skin!

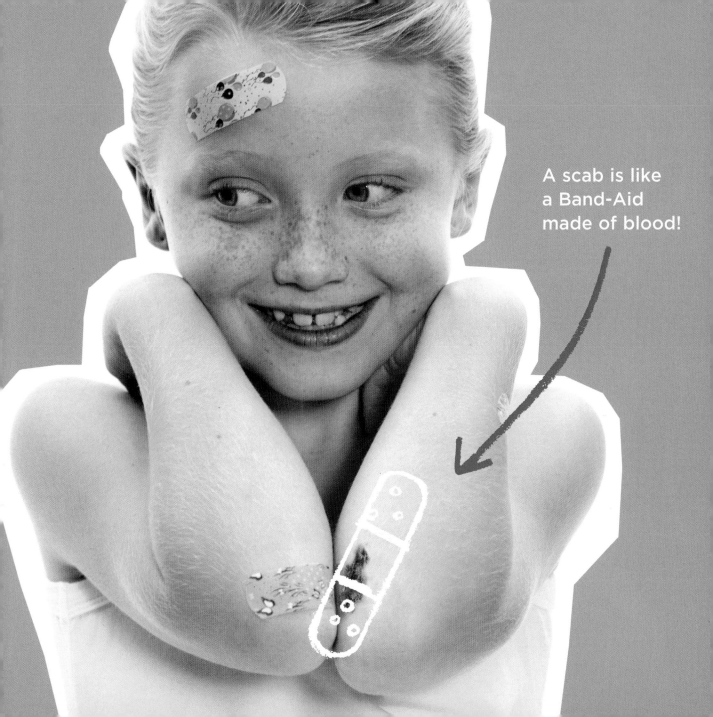

A scab is like
a Band-Aid
made of blood!

Your skin grows as you sleep.

It stretches too!
(baby inside!)

Skin is thick on your hands.
But the skin on the
bottom of your feet
is the thickest.

thick

thickest

thicker

16

It is three layers deep,

Epidermis

about as thick
as a piece
of paper

Dermis

15-40 times
thicker than
the epidermis

Hypodermis

The thickness of this layer
changes from person to person

And feeds an entire zoo!

not this kind!

not this kind!

I eat dead skin!

He may look creepy, but without him and THOUSANDS of his friends we would be up to our eyeballs in dead skin!

Dust mite

this kind!

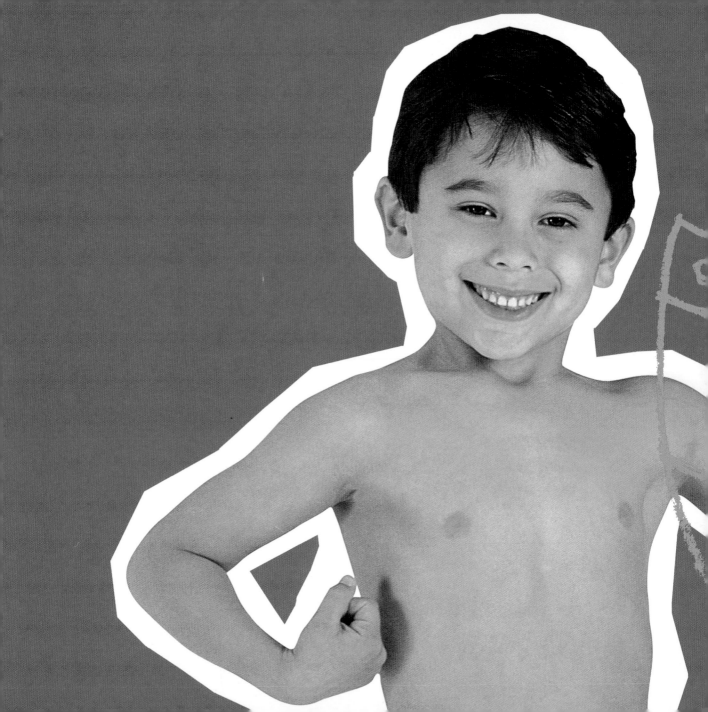

Skin is like a suit of armor.

bacteria

ping!

ping!

Skin stops harmful bacteria from getting inside you.

21

Skin can tell where you've been.

You are leaving fingerprints on this book right now.

This is what a fingerprint
looks like, really close up.

Your feet
make footprints.

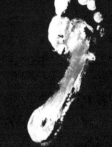

No two fingerprints are the same.
Your finger and footprints are yours alone!

Your brain and heart do their part. But...

brain

heart

can't live without these!

Your brain works with your senses to keep you safe.

25

Your heart sends blood to your brain and skin, keeping them healthy.

...it's your **skin**
that holds you **in!**

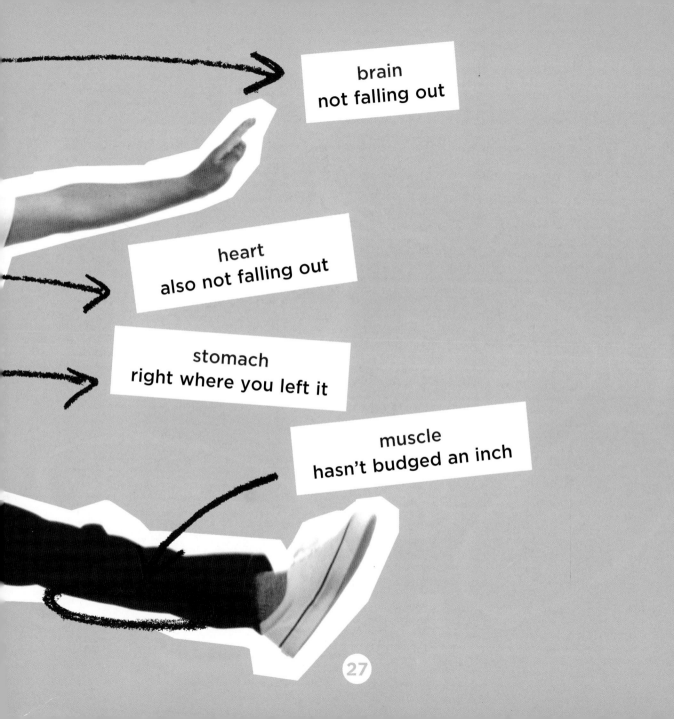

brain
not falling out

heart
also not falling out

stomach
right where you left it

muscle
hasn't budged an inch

Zigzag through these ideas for more thoughts about the skin you're in.

Does a feather feel the same on your nose as on your elbow?

Name all of the colors your skin can turn.

Color your fingertip with washable marker. Press on paper to see your print.

Why are there lines in the skin on your hands?

When you open your eyes, where do your eyelids go?

Why is the skin on your lips a different color than the skin on your nose?

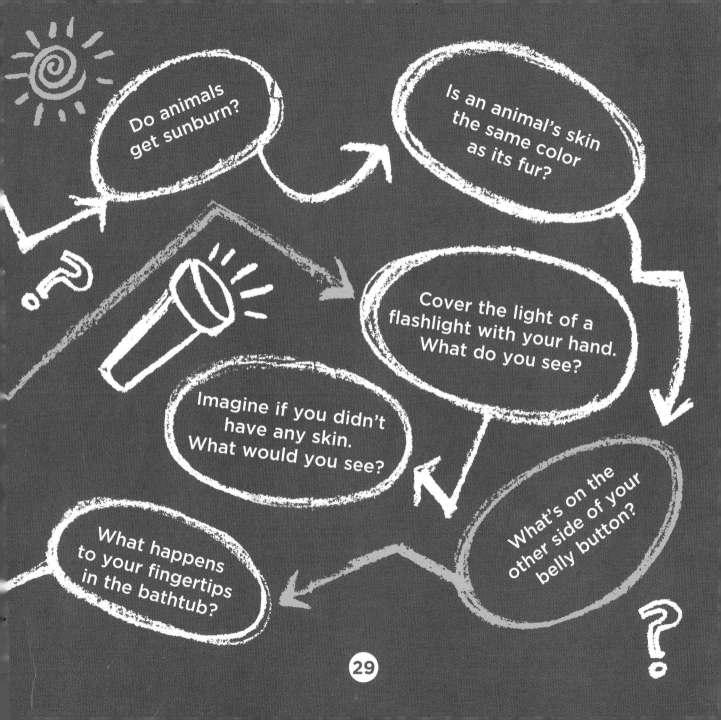

National Geographic's
net proceeds support
vital exploration,
conservation, research,
and education programs.

Published by The National Geographic Society
1145 17th Street, N.W.
Washington, D.C. 20036
Visit us online at www.nationalgeographic.com/books

Design: fuszion

Printed in the United States of America

Library of Congress Cataloging-in-Publication Data

Baines, Rebecca.
  Your Skin Holds You In: A Book About Your Skin /
by Becky Baines.
     p. cm. — (A Zig Zag Book)
  ISBN 978-1-4263-0311-1 (hardcover : alk. paper) —
ISBN 978-1-4263-0312-8
(library binding : alk. paper)
1. Skin — Juvenile literature. I. Title.
QM484.B35 2008
611'.77—dc22
2007044156

Photo Credits
Corbis: 24
Getty: Cover, 4, 6, 8, 11, 12, 14, 15, 17, 19, 25, 26
iStock: 23
PunchStock: 9, 10, 16, 18, 19, 20, 22, 23

To the greatest parents in
the world. Thank you for all
the love and support...
and, of course, the skin I'm in.
—B.B.